So, You're
—A—
MANAGER

DO THE RIGHT THING!
A Practical Guide for Christian and Secular
Leaders in the Workplace

DERRICK SPEARMAN

Scripture taken from the HOLY BIBLE, NEW INTERNATIONAL VERSION®. Copyright © 1973, 1978, 1984 International Bible Society. Used by permission of Zondervan. All rights reserved.

Unless otherwise indicated, all Scripture quotations are taken from the Holy Bible, New Living Translation, copyright 1996, 2004. Used by permission of Tyndale House Publishers, Inc., Wheaton, Illinois 60189. All rights reserved.

"Scripture taken from the New King James Version®. Copyright © 1982 by Thomas Nelson, Inc. Used by permission. All rights reserved. "Certain names used in this book are fictitious names.

Published in the United States of America

"So, You're A Manager" Do the Right Thing!

Houston, Texas Copyright © 2017 by Derrick Spearman Request for information should be directed to the contact page of the Publishing Company's web-site. All rights reserved. No part of this publication may be reproduced, stored in a retrieval system, or transmitted in any form of by any means- electronic, mechanical, recording, or any other – except for brief quotations in printed reviews, without the prior permission of the publisher.

Table of Contents

Introduction...7

Acknowledgements..9

Seed Planting..11

Flow in Your Confidence...16

Tough Times = Test Time...20

Remember...25

Food for Thought...28

Reward Immediately..32

Attacks..35

Managerial Trustworthiness..39

Be Responsible Pass It On...42

Diversity in the Workplace..45

Yes U Can...49

The Invitation...54

Introduction

This book was joyfully written to inspire and encourage managers and supervisors to excel in their workplace leadership role as Godly examples to people they lead. Perhaps you are a manager or maybe you are aspiring to become one. There is always a place for leaders on the job: people who will step up, speak up, and live up to their full potential while at work. The question is what kind of leader would you like to be? One who depends on human earthly knowledge alone or one who consistently decides to trust God in all things. Naturally your company/organization has necessary training tools to assist with your development as a manager, but there is also supernatural assistance available to you. Divine guidance is available through the Holy Scriptures. We have been privileged as a country to have had so many exceptional leaders and we can certainly learn from their leadership expertise, but there is a leader above all leaders. His name is Jesus, and he is the best example we will ever have as he is the only impeccable model for imperfect mankind. I pray that you are helped by this practical guide for Christian and Secular managers in the workplace. Doing the right thing is doing it God's way! Some managers would probably agree that their actual job duty is simple, but figuring out how to deal with various personalities, utilizing sound judgment, and dealing with upper management is probably the most tedious part of a manager's responsibility. Thank God there is always divine assistance available to every leader. All you have to do is ask for it then receive from the one who is right 100% of the time: God sees all, knows all, and is everywhere at the same time. He can handle your problem and my problem simultaneously without error as he speaks from his word.

"The Bible was not given to increase our knowledge but to change our lives". D.L. Moody

Acknowledgements

I want to acknowledge God for his unspeakable gifts which are at work in my life today. I'm also very thankful for my wife's support and the support of my family and friends who consistently and fervently prayed for me during the writing process.

1

SEED PLANTING

To my surprise after a recent reflection, my experience in management totals over thirty years. I have always enjoyed working with people, but I never thought I'd be in supervisory role for such a long period of time: especially after graduating from college with a degree in English. Nevertheless, life as a manager can be both rewarding and quite interesting. By rewarding, I mean I've had numerous opportunities to plant positive seeds of wisdom in the lives of so many people following my leadership. This does not mean I preached, taught the bible to them, or played gospel music for their hearing while in the workplace: rather it means I seized moments of opportunities to take the high road to resolve conflicts and other job-related issues as quickly as possible through integrity and by choosing to be an example of good work ethics. This also doesn't mean that I've been the perfect manager as there are no perfect managers, but there are effective managers. Effective managers continue to evolve. They are always learning. I believe your life is the only church people will sometimes see. Of course, "some seeds fell on stony ground" meaning those positive seeds of integrity, wisdom, and efforts to fairly handle conflicts on the job were not received by some people working on my team; however, those are the same people that kept me praying and focused on my real assignment on earth. By interesting, I mean some employees were both funny and somewhat disappointing at the same time. They would hang-out together during their personal time, eat together during lunch breaks, joke with each other daily, but would viciously verbally attack each other (through back-stabbing) in the manager's booth/office. Needless to say, those office visits were excellent moments for coaching and development: to which I would often emphasize the importance of teamwork and the destruction that gossip and rumors cause.

I've worked on several jobs in my life-time and one of them was quite noteworthy because at that time in my career, I no longer desired to manage people. Consequently, I returned to a managerial role because that's where the money was: yet all the while God was showing me that it really wasn't about me. I say to every Christian manager, remember there is always a bigger picture with God. Christ wants to use you in the workplace to plant spiritual seeds of love, forgiveness, and integrity through the power of the Holy Spirit. Planting Godly seeds is not restricted to verbal preaching or teaching in a traditional churchy environment. Seed planting for every Christian manager involves being a Christ-like example to those you lead and being Christ-like does not always require a verbal announcement. Christianity is a life-style. You may not ever be labeled a Christian by some people, but they will notice a difference in you (which ultimately) makes them inquisitive about your behavior. Of course, if you are a non-Christian manager, the good news is you can become a Christian manager immediately through confession and belief in Jesus Christ. I'll talk about that a little later. From retail to other leadership roles in the secular realm, I never made a habit of telling people that I was a minister, pastor, or even a believer in Christ for that matter. If someone asked me about my faith or church, then of course I would gladly share with those who were asking at the time. The fact is, people eventually concluded or assumed I was a believer in Christ by either seeing me at various church functions or by observing my behavior while at work. One important fact about planting good spiritual seed is, you never know when the seed will start to develop in a person's life. That part is up to God! Some employees including my colleagues would comment occasionally about my demeanor to which I would only smile and say, "thank you." The reality is, I take zero credit for such comments. I give all the praise and glory to

God, and so should you! <u>Consider God's Word</u>:

I Peter 3: 15-16. But in your hearts revere Christ as Lord. Always be prepared to give an answer to everyone who asks you to give the reason for the hope that you have. But do this with gentleness and respect, keeping a clear conscience, so that those who speak maliciously against your good behavior in Christ may be ashamed of their slander.

2

Flow in Your Confidence

I've always liked working in a diverse environment mainly because of the various learning opportunities that come along with it, but my return to a supervisory role automatically activated a level of patience that far superceded the normal amount of patience necessary for working with colleagues and employees in a non-supervisory role. Make no mistake about it, supervising others will require a certain level of patience and understanding that OJT (on the job training) alone cannot offer. OJT is significant and necessary, but Christian managers cannot rely on that alone. Christian managers operate within a standard that is literally out of this world. It's called a kingdom standard, and the kingdom standard travels with you wherever you go. Managers and supervisors (whether Christian or non-Christian) will have opportunities to demonstrate favoritism and/or dishonesty. You may also be blatantly (or perhaps in a subtle way) be invited to participate in other unethical practices like: theft, revenge through employee evaluations, or nit-picking with the intent to pressure subordinates to resign from their position. Whichever the case, never compromise your integrity! You may even feel pressured by corporate executives or upper management to carry out unethical practices, but you don't have to surrender to such pressure. You can choose to do the right thing by doing the following:

1. Flow in your confidence by resisting negativity. Do not lend your ear to foolish counsel and be prepared to lose certain so-called friends or acquaintances when you choose this path.

2. Resist the urge to be a people pleaser. Stay focused by ensuring fairness across the board. The crowed

isn't always right. This stance may not be popular, but God will be pleased with the attitude of your heart

3. Know your rights as an employee. Become familiar with local, state, and governmental laws that pertain to your rights in the workplace. Also know the do's and don'ts of your company or organization.

4. Stay abreast of changing work trends. Change is inevitable so accept it. Read and take advantage of various learning opportunities that offer new steps to various complex problems. Embrace change with a positive attitude.

5. Practice professionalism, respect, and honesty when dealing with those in high ranking authority and when dealing with subordinates. Avoid yelling, profanity, gossip, and other behavior that doesn't align with biblical teaching. Respect other people and their

opinion regarding different social matters because people are entitled to their own opinion.

6. Practice transparency. If you can't do it, say you can't do it. If for some reason you don't understand a process or assignment, communicate that you don't understand. If you have to make adjustments to a rule, communicate that adjustment then tell why the adjustment had to be made.

You can change your workplace atmosphere (for the better) if you follow those steps. Eventually people will respect your decision to consistently demonstrate fairness. Be confident in Christ and trust God for the results!

Consider God's Word: James 4: 7 So whoever knows the right thing to do and fails to do it, for him it is sin.

I John 5:14 This is the confidence we have approaching God: that if we ask anything according to his will, he hears

3

Tough Times = Test Time

Everybody answers to somebody or at least they should. As a matter of fact, God loves hierarchy. Remember both Christian and secular managers are supervised by someone too, and unfortunately a manager can also fall victim to having a person over them who simply wares the title of a supervisor. Please understand as a manager, your conviction to become more like Christ automatically givesway to testing. To that end I say, you will be tested because generally speaking people don't like to hear the truth about themselves: especially if the truth is coming from a subordinate. I believe there's a way to say anything. Managers shouldn't speak to their supervisor in a disrespectful dogmatic manner; however, when it's time communicate the truth regarding a work-related situation don't allow fear to grip your mind and keep you from communicating the truth because it could be your divine assignment at the time. Christians are given boldness in our spiritual walk. Examine your motive by-way of God's word. Ask God for insight and follow God's direction. It's always a good work practice to not address issues of concern when you're angry. Instead, take the time to pray first. Listen to the voice of the Holy Spirit and remain silent until he speaks to you about those sensitive subject matters or major issues of concern on the job. Praying first does not guarantee that your response will be immediately accepted, appreciated, or even spark immediate change. It also doesn't guarantee that your boss won't be offended, but praying first shows your submission to Christ which is God's will. Be assured that God's sustaining grace will carry you through. Following the leadership of the Holy Spirit ensures that God will be glorified in your conversation. You may even experience unfair treatment because of your choice to communicate the facts about a work-related situation, but don't worry because it's always better to have the presence of God "in the fire" than to be "in the fire" without God's presence. As a manager you must be ready to expect the unexpected. You literally must be prepared to deal with sudden directives from superiors via phone calls, in-person, skype or email. If you supervise a team of people, you must also be prepared to deal with call-in's on a daily basis. There are also building/maintenance issues along with customer/client concerns to deal with (if you work in the public sector), but God will provide balance and peace for the process while you focus on putting out unexpected small fires.

You can even smile during times of testing! All of this and much more can be handled without cracking under pressure by remaining calm, being organized, and becoming familiar with company policies and procedures.

Choosing to walk by faith does not mean you are inactive and ignorant while waiting on God to move. Know what's expected of you at all times, and pass your test! Your heavenly father will surround you during times of testing, and he will give you a testimony of victory, so be prepared and do the right thing!

<u>Consider God's Word</u>: Philippians 4:6-7 Do not be anxious about anything, but in everything by prayer and supplication with thanksgiving let your requests be made known to God. And the peace of God, which surpasses all understanding, will guard your hearts and your minds in Christ Jesus.

James 1:12 Blessed is the man who remains steadfast under trial, for when he has stood the test he will receive the crown of life, which God has promised to those who love him.

I Peter 5:10 And after you have suffered a little while, the God of all grace, who has called you to his eternal glory in

Christ, will himself restore, confirm, strengthen, and establish you.

4

Remember!

For those managers who may not believe in Christ, please remember that your non-belief will never cancel out God's powerful presence on earth; nor will it cancel his supernatural ability to cover, protect, and provide for his people. Science is constantly evolving, but one thing remains crystal clear. Scientists will never be able to create a man and breathe breath into his body causing him to become a living soul...why? because some things are reserved for God only. Having said that, also bear in mind that life has a way of (bringing-back to your front door) what you've put out. Christian or not, when you plot against others (whether it's your co-worker, neighbor, friend, family member, or your supervisor), sooner or later someone will do the same to you, and it won't feel good. The world's greatest gospel singer Mahalia Jackson said, "If you dig one ditch you better dig two cause the trap you set just may be for you". Mahalia's quote actually aligns with God's Word in Psalm 7: 15-16 which says "He makes a pit, digging it out and falls into the hole that he has made: the trouble he causes recoils on himself; his violence comes down on his own head". As a supervisor, remember also that professional boundaries are necessary. Not everyone will like you, and that's ok. Aristotle said "a friend to everyone is a friend to no one". Over the years I've consistently stated to those following my leadership on the job "I will always treat the team in a fair acceptable manner that's my promise to you". Effective managers understand the importance of treating everybody the same. Even if you have a favorite person on the team, Godly wisdom will teach you how to handle that person in the workplace so that other people are not mis-treated. Do the right thing! Remember, God's word will stand even when everything else has crumbled.

Consider God's Word: James 3:17 But the wisdom that comes from heaven is first of all pure; then peace-loving, considerate, submissive, full of mercy and good fruit, impartial and sincere.

5

Food for Thought

Successful managers also know the importance of building a team. Team members are essential to any organization, and managers must be willing to listen to their team members. This of course assumes that team members are reasonable and mindful of overall goals and expectations of the company or organization. Team members help you to understand that you don't know it all. They bring valuable input to the table, and they may eventually have your back if necessary. When you make a mistake as a manager, acknowledge your mistake as soon as possible. Doing so helps your team to see that you don't think too highly of yourself. It also helps to build trust and respect amongst the team. If you don't know the answer about a particular matter or subject, express that to the team and assure them that you will find the answer. Being knowledgeable about your job duty is necessary, but it doesn't mean you have all the answers all the time. Never be close-minded about learning a new technique from a colleague or even from a subordinate. I recall working with a colleague many years ago (in retail) who was extremely poor at supervising others. This person was a know-it-all type of manager and overly proud about her accomplishments. Unfortunately, this manager treated her team like they were irreversibly ignorant. Employees working under her leadership were micro-managed and were often robotic during her presence at the store. It wasn't a pleasant work environment. At the time my assignment to that location was temporary as I eventually moved on, but I felt empathy for the people who remained under that type of leadership. Food for thought: I was temporarily placed in that environment so that I could intercede for that manager and for the people on that team. Of course, employees have rights too. They can report abuse of power and other possible work-related infractions, but that wasn't my assignment at the time. God wanted me to intercede for people on that team, and he wanted me to let his light shine through my behavior and my response. The reality is I could have used my influence in a negative manner by participating in negative conversations and finger-pointing, but thank God I eventually chose to pray because my first reaction was to immediately bail. I also made sure to re-direct sales associates (to that manager) for one on one conversations in an effort to resolve issues. After leaving that store, I later received a phone call telling me how my presence there brought so much peace to the environment. Another employee from that location told me (in person) that my presence would be missed and that my behavior helped them to see things in a different light. Praise God! You may also be placed in a similar situation as Christian leader. If so, do the right thing! Focus on the larger picture because it's never about you!

Consider God's Word:

Luke 6:28 bless those who curse you, pray for those who mistreat you

Galatians 6:3 For if anyone thinks he is something when he is nothing, he deceives himself.

Proverbs 28: 25 An arrogant man stirs up strife, But he who trusts in the LORD will prosper.

6

Reward Immediately

When an employee does something commendable, you should acknowledge that employee immediately if possible. If you can't immediately speak with the employee about their positive response/behavior, do it as soon as possible because that employee deserves to hear it, and they may be expecting you to acknowledge them. Never wait on annual evaluations to acknowledge an employees' good performance. Your acknowledgement can be a handwritten note, an announcement to the team, or a simple email. You should also (as much as possible) involve those you supervise in the decision-making process regarding optional matters such as holiday celebrations or staff birthday celebrations etc. It's also good to appreciate employees by occasionally having snacks, lunch, or giving small tokens of appreciation that include the entire team. Include those employees who may not deserve it because the hope is they will eventually be motivated to improve. Of course, employees who consistently perform in a sub-standard manner can infect the entire team. Your duty as a manager or supervisor is to address those patterns of behavior or poor performance through training, coaching, or disciplinary procedures provided by your company or organization. Even if work separation (for that employee) is deemed necessary, you can take comfort in knowing that you've done everything possible to help guide that employee into job compliance. I learned early-on from a manager in the 1990's that employees fire themselves. Do the right thing regardless of an employee's great performance or lack thereof.

<u>Consider God's Word</u>: Matthew 7: 12 So whatever you wish that others would do to you, do also to them, for this is the Law and the Prophets.

Ephesians: 4:32 Be kind to one another, tenderhearted, forgiving one another, as God in Christ forgave you.

Philippians 2:3 Do nothing from selfishness or empty conceit, but with humility of mind regard one another as more important than yourselves.

7

Attacks

My late pastor Reverend C.A Berry would often say, "If the devil ain't bothering you, chances are he probably already has you." Whether the attack is verbal or physical, no one likes to be attacked. Don't be surprised when people attack you for no reason. Jesus said "if they hate you remember they hated me first". We live in a corrupt world and just like carrying his name automatically gives way to testing, carrying his name also gives way to all kinds of undeserved evil attacks. At times, God may allow you to see an attack before it happens through a dream or he may use a prophet or pastor to speak to you. Whichever method God decides to use, never take-on the battle in the flesh. One blessing that every believer has is we NEVER have to fight our battles with carnal weapons. The Lord will fight for us when we choose to fight his way. If you are blind-sided by an attack or if you see an attack coming-on, go into immediate spiritual warfare by putting on spiritual gear.

What do I mean?

1) when people believe gossip about you;

2) when those you supervise speak evil of your goodwill;

3) when you endeavor to treat everybody on the team in a fair acceptable manner but no one seemingly appreciates your efforts;

4) when other people are chosen for the promotion but you were better qualified;

5) if you are wrongfully retaliated against;

6) if your supervisor seeks to turn other colleagues against you;

7) If other colleagues are acknowledged for their work contributions, but you aren't acknowledged for your work contributions;

If any or all of these attacks come against you, remember that your real enemy is Satan, and he also uses people. I know you wish everybody was saved like you, but the reality is there are non-believers sitting in high ranking positions on the job (that's ok) because God sometimes allows it for some reason. Just keep in mind that God sits on the highest throne, and he always has the final say! Another good thing about prayer is, you can pray to God without ever opening your mouth or ever getting on your knees. God will hear your prayer and come to your rescue in due time, so don't fight with revenge, profanity, or idleness. Fight with faith and prayer because they are both powerful intangible spiritual weapons. I have experienced the pain of choosing to fight battles in the flesh, and the results were always disappointing. God will help you to do the right thing (as you seek him for direction) during your season of attack.

Consider God's Word:

2 Thessalonians 3:3 But the Lord is faithful, and he will strengthen you and protect you from the evil one.

1 Peter 5:8-9 Be alert and of sober mind. Your enemy the devil prowls around like a roaring lion looking for someone to devour. Resist him, standing firm in the faith, because you know that the family of believers throughout the world is undergoing the same kind of sufferings.

Romans 8:31 What then shall we say to these things? If God is for us, who can be against us?

8

Managerial Trustworthiness

It's a fact, when people trust your leadership they tend to share things with you occasionally. It may be personal or sometimes employees simply need to vent about a particular matter on the job. Don't be tensed, too busy, or afraid to listen because it's actually a compliment to your character when they ask to speak with you confidentially. Imagine my relief (when earlier in my career) I found that all I needed to do was listen when those moments came. Never divulge confidential conversations with other employees because it destroys managerial trust. Occasionally, I've had to redirect and refer employees to other resources, but most of the time the employee simply wanted the listening ear of a trustworthy leader. Employees who needed a listening ear were given my undivided attention, and they were satisfied with that alone. It was amazing! On another note, you may advance to a managerial position that does not require you to clock-in or out. Praise God for the promotion, and don't abuse that privilege. Arrive to work on time each day, and don't be guilty of constantly leaving work early. God is not the only person watching. Your team is also watching, so do the right thing by setting good work examples for the entire team. You'll be glad you did. Lastly, never talk about an employee (in a negative manner) to another employee. This too destroys the trust factor, and it contributes to low morale on the job. It could even eventually be used as weapon against your character and leadership capabilities.

Consider God's Word:

Proverbs 10: 9 Whoever walks in integrity walks securely,

but he who makes his ways crooked will be found out.

Proverbs 28: 6 Better is a poor man who walks in his integrity than a rich man who is crooked in his ways.

Proverbs 11:13 Whoever goes about slandering reveals secrets, but he who is trustworthy in spirit keeps a thing covered.

Titus 2:7 Show yourself in all respects to be a model of good works, and in your teaching show integrity, dignity...

9

Be Responsible: Pass It On

You may as well accept the fact, managers are always on duty in a sense (even when it's your day off) because managers are responsible for whatever goes on with your team or facility at all times. For example, if something happens on your day off, you may be required to document, communicate with your superiors, conduct follow-ups, or address the matter with those you supervise upon your return to work. That being the case, act responsibly and train others on the team to communicate and address certain matters in your absence. As a pastor I've said on many occasions, I haven't done a good job of pastoral ship if no one has been trained to carry-on in my absence. Don't be selfish or intimidated. Pass on your knowledge by ensuring that your team is cross-trained (meaning other employees can carry out certain work duties) while another employee on the team is absent. Inform your team about the necessity for everyone to be cross-trained and follow through with that requirement. You should also be true to your feelings if you are sensing that it's time to retire from your position. Many people stay on the job (even though they are financially secured for retirement), while remaining rigid and self-absorbed thinking they are irreplaceable. If that's you, please know that you are always replaceable no matter how well your job performance is. On the contrary, decide to gracefully pass the torch when it's your time to go. Don't allow the company or organization to decide for you because they could eventually do so through a process of elimination.

"The task of the leader is to get their people from where they are to where they have not been." Henry Kissinger

Consider God's Word:

James 1:5 If any of you lacks wisdom, let him ask God, who gives generously to all without reproach, and it will be given him.

Psalm 119:66 Teach me good judgment and knowledge, for I believe in your commandments.

Proverbs 16:22 Good sense is a fountain of life to him who has it, but the instruction of fools is folly.

10

Diversity in the Workplace

No matter what your cultural back ground may be, God loves you. Since God loves people, we must exemplify *agape* love which is God's love for us. We should praise God for diversity in the world and workplace because God created the human race. No ethnic group is superior to the other. No culture is superior to another. Be conscious of cultural differences and generational gaps in the workplace such as: Traditionalist (1945 and prior), Baby Boomers (1946-1964), Generation X (1965-1979), Millennials (1980-1994), and Generation Z (1995 and later). All of these groups bring something different and valuable to the table. As a supervisor, you have the exciting task of ensuring all groups flow in an effective productive manner as coordinating parts. As the leader, you should respect all cultural differences on your team and encourage your team to do the same. People learn in different ways. To name a couple of ways, some people are visual learners. They need to see it in graphs, charts, or diagrams: while some people are auditory learners: they learn through listening. Whatever the learning type may be, respect is key word. A mutual respect amongst team members, helps to enable the team to mesh together for the purpose of achieving work goals. Observe the various work tasks of your team and the areas they may shine best in. For example, Sally-Beth may be great at greeting clients as they enter the front door. She loves to greet people, but she rarely gets the opportunity to do so because most of the time she is scheduled for a duty that she really doesn't shine best in. Think about utilizing Sally-Beth in the work area she loves most and would shine best in. The outcome can be rewarding for the entire team and even the entire company or organization. Another good idea (as I stated early) is to occasionally have a team lunch or breakfast to bring employees together away from the work area to stimulate conversation amongst the team. This will help to break barriers in communication as team members will eventually begin to value each other which directly affects morale. Morale is a BIGGIE! High morale levels in the workplace help to boost productivity. It may sound crazy, but your team can actually enjoy workplace productivity. After all, productivity is very significant. Your company may offer guidelines/trainings on the topic to further assist you. If not, perhaps you can suggest a training on the subject.

<u>Consider God's Word</u>: 1 John 4:7-8 Beloved, let us love one another, for love is from God, and whoever loves has been born of God and knows God. Anyone who does not love does not know God, because God is love.

John 3:16 For God so loved the world, that he gave his only Son, that whoever believes in him should not perish but have eternal life

48

11

Yes, U Can

One of the worse things a leader can do is to not take a vacation. Both employees and managers need to occasionally get away from the job. Don't make the mistake of thinking the company/organization can't do without you for a few days. The company probably existed prior to your arrival, and it certainly won't cease to exist while you are on vacation a few days. Vacations are designed for times of refreshing and enjoyment. You should also know when to stay at home if you are sick. People don't function @ 100% when they are sick or exhausted; furthermore, if you're illness is contagious chances are you could spread your illness to others. Use your judgment and follow your company's procedures regarding vacation/sick usage and utilize that time when it's necessary. Yes you can take vacation and sick time when it's necessary. If you are working for a small business/organization, speak to your supervisor about possibly taking time off. On another note, dealing with job demands, constant small fires, overwhelming feelings of day to day operations, dealing with internal/external complaints, emergencies, and much more can rob you of smile and your laughter if you allow it. You may not feel like smiling, but I want to encourage you to smile anyway. Smiles are potent expressions as they often communicate our feelings. Did you know that the bible encourages us to smile? The bible says, "a cheerful look brings joy to the heart". If you are a pessimistic person, try changing your view through the power of God's word because your pessimistic view is robbing you of your inner and outer smile. Choose to appreciate life, health, strength, opportunity, free-will, friends, and family: then surround yourself with people who do the same.

Let's have a little Q & A session:

Q. can i genuinely smile at a person who knowingly belittle's me behind my back?

A. yes u can

Q. can i change my negative attitude about my colleagues and supervisor

A. yes u can

Q. can I trust God to give me what i need just when i need it most while on the job?

A. yes u can

Q. can i genuinely give 100% when everyone else on the team is slacking?

A. yes u can

Q. can i really forgive a person who consistently attempts to take credit for my hard work?

A. yes u can

Q. can i control my anger even when I have a right to be angry?

A. yes u can

Q. can i give a hug when i actually need a hug myself?

A. yes u can

Q. can I change my work language to ensure that others are not offended?

A. yes u can

Q. can I stop gossiping and listening to gossip?

A. yes u can

All of this can be done through God's grace. God wants his children to experience the trans-formational power of the

Holy Spirit for all levels of their lives on earth. We will not need the supernatural transformational power of the Holy Spirit in heaven. Decide to experience this change in your life right now!

Consider God's Word:

Ecclesiastes 3: 12-13 I know that there is nothing better for people than to be happy and to do good while they live: that everyone should eat and drink and take pleasure in all his toil—this is God's gift to man.

Isaiah 43:19 See I am doing a new thing; now it springs up! Do you not perceive it?

Psalm 119: 18 Open my eyes that I may see wonderful things about your law.

12

The Invitation

Just as educators in a classroom, managers also have the opportunity to positively impact others in the workplace. Managers have the power to spark change in the people they lead. Like it or not, everybody is influenced by someone. This chapter is an invitation to every non-Christian manager or supervisor to surrender their body, mind, and spirit to the person Jesus Christ. Christ extends a personal invitation to everyone in need of a savior. He doesn't invite you to spend eternity separated from him in hell. There is but one perfect model for mankind to follow, and that perfect model is now seated at the right hand of his father praying for you because he loves you. He is the relevant perfect example for your home, your workplace, your community, the church, and the entire world. Perhaps you've made some dumb choices at work as a leader. Join the club! None of us are perfect. If you're a good manager, you can become a better one by learning from your mistakes through the power of acknowledgement and repentance. The truth is (from a spiritual perspective), without the power of Christ operating in your life, you're simply existing at work not living. When you're living for Christ, your desire is point people in the direction of spiritual change which ultimately leads to eternal life with Jesus Christ. The bible tells us to "Trust in the Lord with all of our hearts and lean not to our own understanding". Become a better leader today by following workplace guidelines consistently and by submitting yourself under the authority of Christ. "Confess with your mouth and believe in your heart that God raised him (Jesus) from the dead; and you shall be saved". From that point on, your entire focus will change as you are anointed for his work.

Be determined to walk in humility and make every effort to treat people the way God would have you treat them. It's also important that you join a bible believing Christ centered congregation because your spiritual growth depends on it. Connect and stay connected to a small group and serve in that ministry. Visit the sick, visit those in prison, give to the poor, demonstrate love, pray for others, obey, follow leadership, and share the gospel with non-believers. You'll be glad you did.

I truly hope you were helped by this practical guide to becoming the leader God wants you to become. May God continue to bless you with his wisdom as you endeavor to lead people in the workplace, church, community, social group, or in the classroom. Please visit our website www.allwelcomechurch.org for information about our church.

www.ingramcontent.com/pod-product-compliance
Lightning Source LLC
Chambersburg PA
CBHW070957240526
45469CB00016B/1549